D1483498

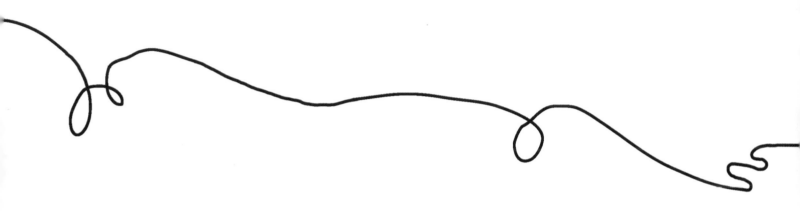

Puppets Unlimited with Everyday Materials
Copyright © 2019 Tara Books Pvt. Ltd.

For the text: Gita Wolf, Anushka Ravishankar,
Ragini Siruguri, Dhwani Shah and Rohini Srinivasan
For the photographs: Ragini Siruguri
For the illustrations: Dhwani Shah

For this edition:
Tara Books Pvt. Ltd., India < www.tarabooks.com >
and
Tara Publishing Ltd., UK < www.tarabooks.com/uk >

Design: Ragini Siruguri
Production: C. Arumugam

Thanks to DakshinaChitra, Chennai
for the photographs on pages 106, 107, 108 and 112

Printed in India by Canara Traders and Printers Pvt. Ltd.

All rights reserved. No part of this work may be reproduced in
any form without the prior written permission of the publisher.

ISBN 978-93-83145-66-9

PUPPETS UNLIMITED

with everyday materials

GITA WOLF • ANUSHKA RAVISHANKAR

RAGINI SIRUGURI • DHWANI SHAH • ROHINI SRINIVASAN

Anything can be turned into a PUPPET...

You just need to know how!

What is a puppet?

A puppet is a doll that can be made to move. The use of puppets in a theatrical performance is called 'puppetry'. Puppetry involves two interesting things. One is making the puppets. The other is making them act. A puppet show is one of the most fun things to put up – and to watch!

So what's this book about?

We show you how to make your own puppets, using all kinds of stuff that you find around you. We think there's no limit to the type of puppets you can make, and the kind of materials you can turn into puppets. This is what we found out when we made puppets.

The main point is this: your puppet needs to work, to move in the way you want it to. So when you go through this book, remember that any puppet you make doesn't have to look exactly like ours, but you do need to pay careful attention to how we made each puppet, and how it works. Apart from that, just go right ahead and follow your own ideas!

CANS & TINS

RECYCLED STRAWS

TOILET PAPER ROLLS

GOOGLY EYES

SCISSORS

BOTTLE CAPS

PENCILS

Digging up things

So this is how we started: each of us went home and looked for materials with which to make our puppets. We dug through old cupboards and wastepaper baskets for all kinds of things. We even searched outside and found natural materials that could become puppets.

UTENSILS

NEWSPAPER STICKS

PAINT

PAINTBRUSHES

GLUE

SHINY PATTERNED PAPER

COCONUT SHELLS

LEAVES

MARKERS

PAPER CLIPS

SKETCH PENS

TWISTED WIRE BRAIDED WITH WOOL

BEADS AND SHELLS

RIBBON

THERMOCOL BALLS

COLOURED PAPER

THREAD

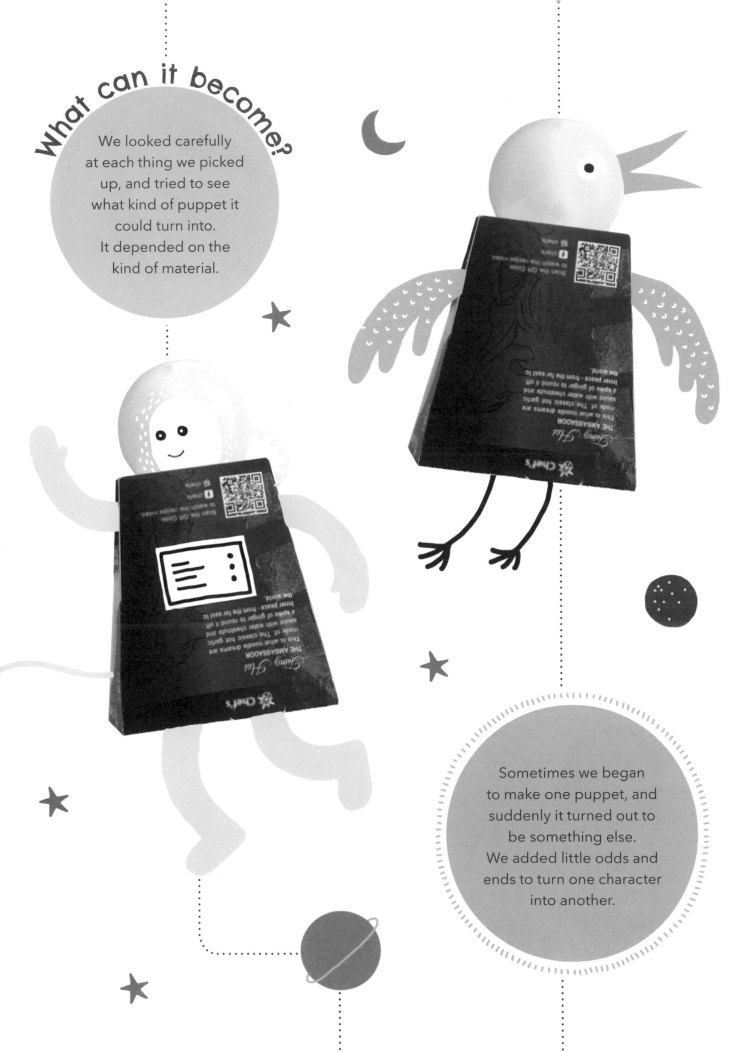

what can it become?

We looked carefully
at each thing we picked
up, and tried to see
what kind of puppet it
could turn into.
It depended on the
kind of material.

Sometimes we began
to make one puppet, and
suddenly it turned out to
be something else.
We added little odds and
ends to turn one character
into another.

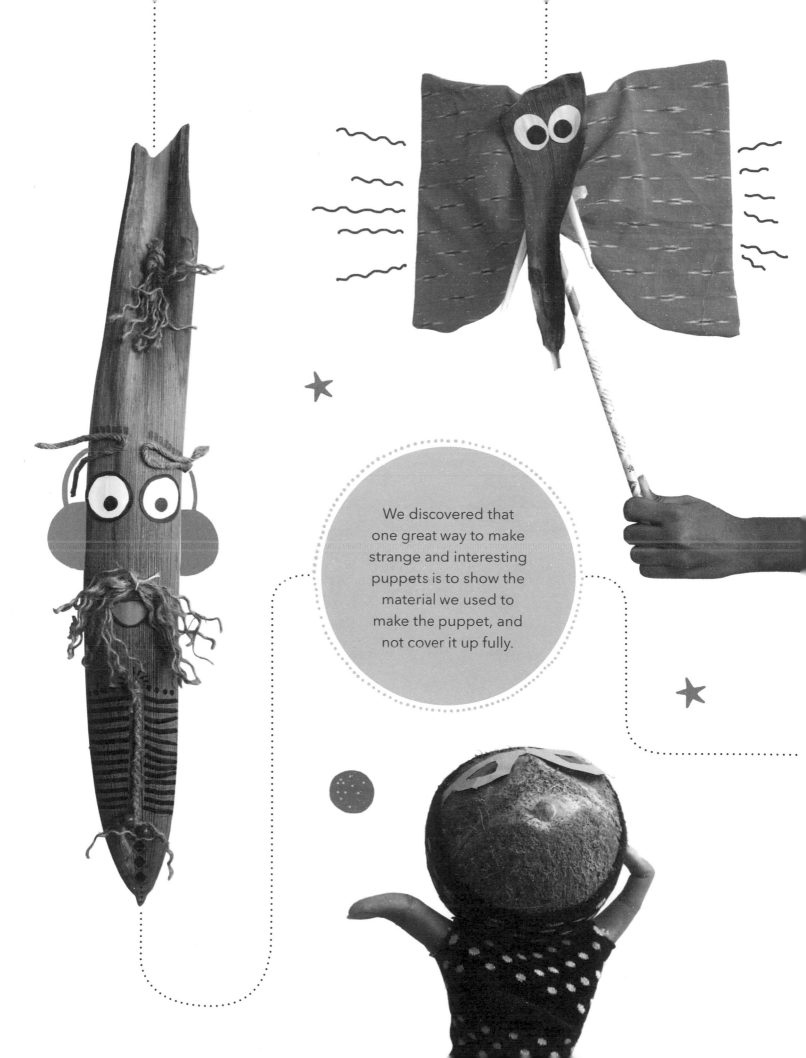

We discovered that one great way to make strange and interesting puppets is to show the material we used to make the puppet, and not cover it up fully.

Names

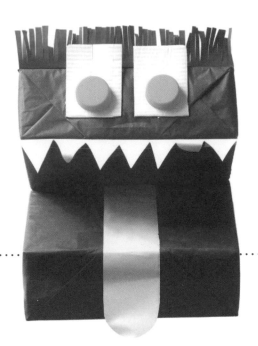

Every puppet we made looked different. Each was a character, quite unique in the way it looked and moved. And we decided therefore to give each puppet a name – going by what it was made of, how it looked, and what it did. 'Chatter-box', for instance, got its name because it was made from a box, and you could make it talk all the time.

Stories

Naming a puppet creates a character. If you change the name, a puppet can become another character. Names can also lead to funny, interesting stories, as they did when we started to get our puppets to 'talk' to each other.

A puppet play

Once we had a set of puppets, we came up with a story and put up a play. Our playscript is included in this book. Try it out or make your own!

And finally, this book...

To make the puppets and their worlds come alive, we've added some fun illustrations. You can use them as cues while making your own. And remember you don't have to look for objects that are exactly like the ones we have used. Adapt and innovate — remember that anything can be turned into a puppet... you just need to know how!

Hand Puppets

Rod Puppets

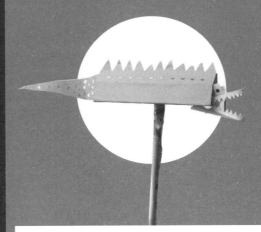

Shadow Puppets

String Puppets

HAND PUPPETS

How do they work?

Hand puppets are some of the simplest puppets to make. You move the puppet using your hands or fingers.

Tiny hand puppets, which are worn on the fingers, are called finger puppets. You can wear a finger puppet on each finger, so you can handle as many as 10 puppets! If your hand puppet is made of a glove or a sock, its face can be twisted to have lots of different expressions.

Another kind of hand puppet is called a clapper-mouth puppet. The mouth of the puppet can be 'clapped' open and shut.

What is special about hand puppets?

They are easy to make and operate. Clapper-mouth puppets are fun to use in performances where there is a lot of conversation.

What did we do?

We made our hand puppets using old socks, coconut shells, balls, paper cups and anything else we could lay our hands on. We made heads out of plastic bottles and paper balls, and bodies out of toilet paper rolls (even rolled-up cardboard glued nicely will do).

Fussy Baker

This character is particular about what he wears. Is he as fussy in his kitchen or is he messy?

☆ ☆ 🧁 ☆ ☆

To make

1 Wrap a **PLASTIC BALL** in **CLOTH** to make the head.

2 For the body, use a **CARDBOARD BOX** of any shape. Cut out two holes on either side, to stick your fingers through. Attach the cloth-covered plastic ball to the top of your box.

18

3   To make a cap, wrap a **TOILET PAPER ROLL** with cloth and glue it onto the head.

4   Cut out eyes and a bushy moustache from **BLACK PAPER** and glue them on. You can add a nose and mouth too!

5   Wrap spotless **WHITE CLOTH** around the box. Now you have before you a clean and crisp Baker!

To move

Slip your hand into the box, stick your fingers through the holes on either side and shake the Baker from side to side. How does he manage to bake?

On your own

Give the Baker a new moustache. Make sure it does not interfere with his cooking!

6   The Baker likes to be clean, so make sure you give him an apron.

Drink-Seller

A cup for a head and bottle caps for a hat make for an ideal drink seller. Maybe he can also hold a straw?

To make

1 Turn a **PAPER CUP** upside down. This is the head.

2 Wear a **SOCK** on your hand and attach the inverted cup to the closed end of the sock.

3 Make two holes in the sock, one on each side, to put your fingers through.

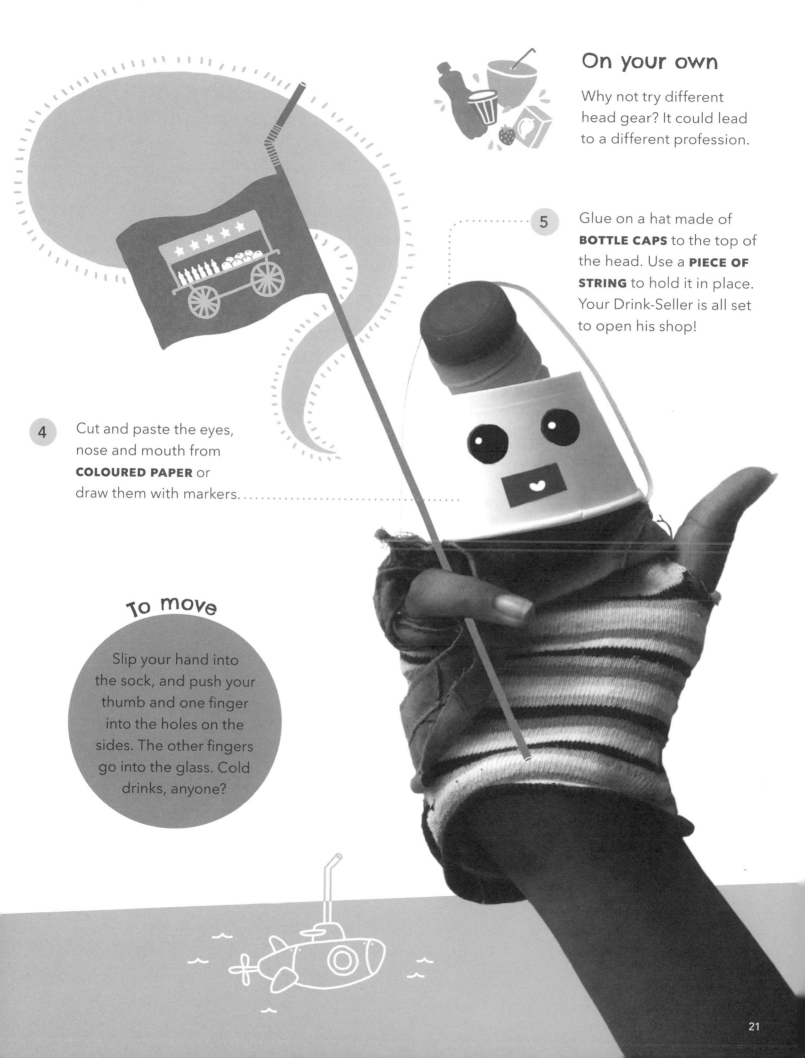

On your own

Why not try different head gear? It could lead to a different profession.

5 Glue on a hat made of **BOTTLE CAPS** to the top of the head. Use a **PIECE OF STRING** to hold it in place. Your Drink-Seller is all set to open his shop!

4 Cut and paste the eyes, nose and mouth from **COLOURED PAPER** or draw them with markers.

To move

Slip your hand into the sock, and push your thumb and one finger into the holes on the sides. The other fingers go into the glass. Cold drinks, anyone?

Tale-Tellers

These two balloon-headed friends speak in whispers and tell tales.

To make

1 Blow up **TWO BALLOONS** and tie them up tightly with **STRING**. Cut **NEWSPAPER** into small strips and glue them onto the balloons in layers. Leave a small patch uncovered at the nape of the neck, enough to stick your fingers through.
Let this dry overnight.

2 Once the newspaper layer is fully dry, you will find that it is hard, while the balloon has shrunk. Remove the balloon from inside by bursting it. Your balloon heads are ready.

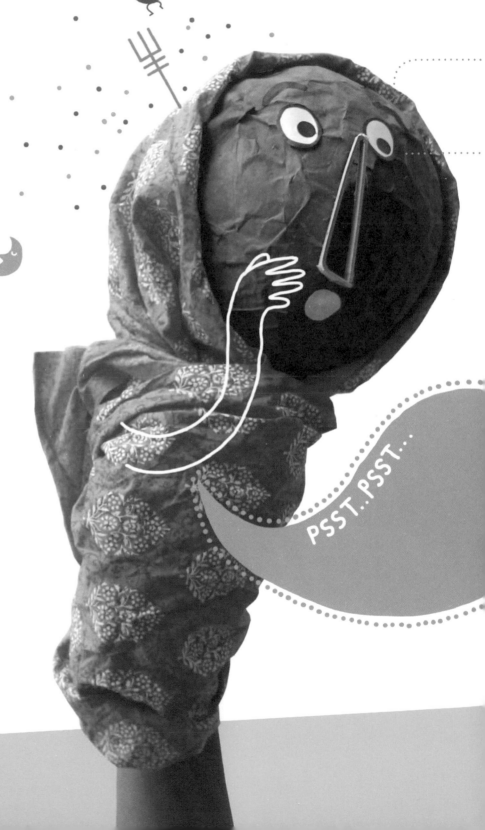

PSST..PSST...

On your own

Uncover the balloon heads. Add green, orange or purple hair. You may want bottle caps for eyes. Fix the balloons onto sticks and turn the Tale-Tellers into young punks!

3 Paint the two heads using **BRIGHT PAINTS**.

4 Cut out eyes from **WHITE PAPER** and glue them on the head. Use a **MARKER** to draw on other features. Make a nose out of a **STRIP OF CARDBOARD**.

5 Drape **PIECES OF CLOTH** over the balloons and pin them in place with **SAFETY PINS**, leaving the faces uncovered. These balloon heads love to talk! And they can tell such tales.

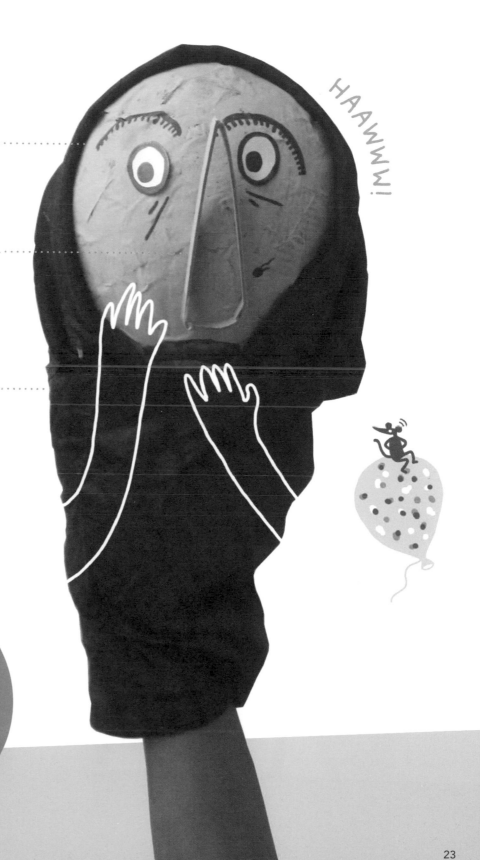

HAAWW!

To move

Stick your fingers through the opening at the base of each of the balloons. When you move your hands, the Tale-Tellers will knowingly wag their balloon-heads up and down.

Mr Big-Ears

With his floppy ears and one eye, is this a sinister magician or a stand-up comedian?

To make

1. Turn a **TIN CAN** upside down. This is the head. Make sure it doesn't have a sharp edge.

2. Wrap the tin can with **PAPER** or **CLOTH**.

Turn Mr Big-Ears into Ms Long-Nose, Mr Rabbit-Teeth, Dr Goggle-Eyes...

3 Cut out ears from **THICK CARD** and glue them on loosely. Use **COLOURED PAPER** or **SKETCH PENS** for the eyes, nose and mouth.

4 Use a colourful **PIECE OF CLOTH** and dress Mr Big-Ears nicely.

To move

Slip your hand under the cloth and into the tin, and move it. Mr Big-Ears will obligingly flap his ears.

CLAP

CLAP

CLAP

25

Sock Croc

Who says socks need to stay on your feet?

To make

1 Glue or stitch together **A PAIR OF SOCKS** in such a way that the open ends are fixed together together along one side for half the length of the socks.

2 Cut out jagged teeth from **COLOURED PAPER** or **CARDBOARD** and glue them along the remaining length of the socks, upto the toe-ends.

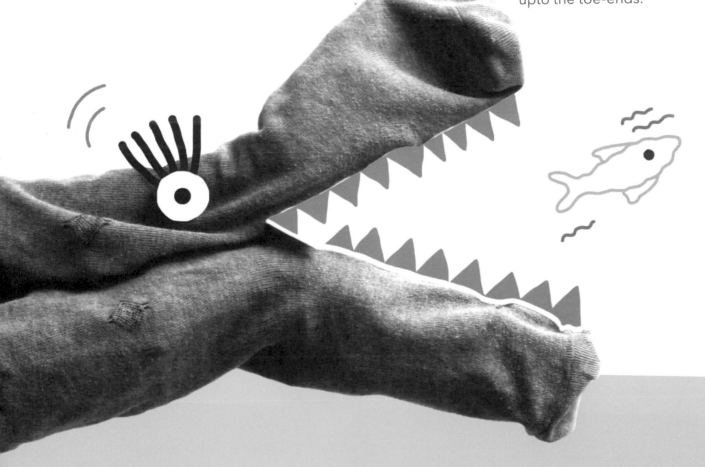

On your own

Two socks don't always have to make a crocodile. Slip the pair of socks on your hands, and try moving your hands in different ways. What do you see? A blooming flower? A Venus flytrap?

3 Use **BOTTLE CAPS** for eyes, and glue them onto the top of one of the socks. Cut and stick eyelashes using **PAPER**. Your pair of socks has become a Croc!

To move

Slip a hand into each sock, keeping one arm above the other. Then move them apart and together. With its jaws open wide, your crocodile is ready for its prey.

Spook

A harmless looking paper cup and a drab piece of cloth are all it takes to make a scary Spook.

To make

1 Turn a **PAPER CUP** upside down to use as a head (and face).

2 Cover the head with **OLD CLOTH** and pin it up with **SAFETY PINS** to keep it in place. Glue the cup and cloth together, but make sure you leave the face exposed. You have quite a spook on your hands!

On your own

Here are some more eerie ideas: Make a pointy hat for your puppet and decide if you want your Spook to turn into a wizard or a witch. What would you get if you covered a white cup with white cloth?

boo!

3 Draw eyes and a mouth with **SKETCH PENS**.

4 Cut holes in the cloth for your fingers to come through.

To move

Wrap the cloth around your hand but in a way that lets you stick your thumb and little finger out through the holes. Push your other fingers into the cup and use them to move the head. The Spook is all set to terrify the public.

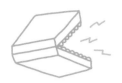

Chatter-box

What else would you call a cut-open cardboard box with moving jaws?

To make

1 Take a **CARDBOARD CARTON** and cut it in half, leaving one broad side intact. Fold the top and bottom halves downwards.

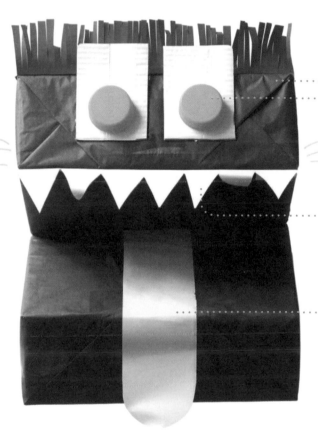

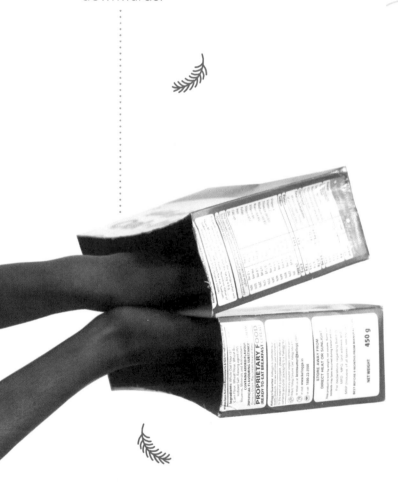

On your own

Chatter-boxes can take many forms. A hungry lion? A barking dog? A yawning hippo?

2 Wrap the **CARTON** with **COLOURED PAPER**.

3 For the eyes, stick **BOTTLE CAPS** on the top half. Cut out **BITS OF BLACK PAPER** for dotting the eyes and for the eyebrows.

4 Cut out a jagged strip of **WHITE PAPER**. Glue it on the mouth. These are the teeth.

5 Cut a long tongue out of **COLOURED PAPER** and glue it into the mouth. This box is ready for a chat!

To move

Place one hand into the lower half and the other hand into the upper half of the carton. Now the jaws can be moved easily, so the box can chatter.

31

General Cap-Tin

A plain old tin became General Cap-tin when he got his moustache and hat. This was the fastest promotion in military history.

To make

1 Turn a **TIN CAN** upside down and wrap it in **COLOURED PAPER**.

2 Cut out facial features from **PAPER** and glue them onto the tin. Add a **PAIR OF GLASSES** for the dignified look.

LEFT.. LEFT... LEFT RIGHT LEFT... LEFT RIGHT LEFT...

3 Make a hat from **BLACK CARDBOARD** or **CHART PAPER** and glue it on.

4 Make a military moustache out of **BLACK CLOTH** and glue it on. The Cap-Tin is now a General!

On your own

Because of his lightning-fast promotion, the General lacks a proper military wardrobe. Perhaps you could supply him with a uniform, stripes, medals and cap. Quick, or else he could get demoted!

To move

Drape the cloth over your hand and insert your hand into the tin. Move your hand from side to side, and the General will move stiffly, like a true military gentleman.

Antarctic Explorer

Torn socks and cellophane paper turned a plain coconut into an adventurous explorer.

To make

1 Use **HALF A COCONUT SHELL** to make the face of the puppet.

2 Fit the open end of a **SOCK** snugly around the back of the coconut shell.

3 Cut out bits of **COLOURED PAPER** and glue them onto the front of the coconut to make goggles. Use **STRIPS OF CELLOPHANE** paper for lens. Your homely nut has become an intrepid Antarctic Explorer!

On your own

Turn the Antarctic Explorer into a ferocious tiger. Try using yellow socks, black paint and paper. Or paint a white sock with yellow and black stripes to create your tiger.

4 Make two holes in the sock for your fingers.

5 To wear the sock, cut open the closed end so you can slip your hand through.

To move

Put your hand through the hole at the bottom of the sock, and insert one finger into each of the two holes. Your fingers become the hands of the explorer. Off to the Antarctic!

Dancing Donkey

Who says donkeys need to be meek? This one turned out to be a great dancer.

To make

1 Take a plastic bottle and using a **CUTTER**, cut off its base. Wrap **TAPE** over the cut edges – so that the cut edges don't hurt your hands.

2 Cut off the top portion of another **SMALLER PLASTIC BOTTLE**.

3 Remove the lid from the bigger bottle. Near the top of the smaller bottle, cut a hole as big as the mouth of the bigger bottle.

4 Stick the first bottle through the hole in the second one, and screw the cap in through the inside of the second bottle. You have an animal structure in place.

On your own

Why not turn the donkey into a zebra? All it needs are stripes. Or paste paper cones as humps on the body, and you have a camel.

5 Mix **BROWN PAINT** with a bit of water and paint both the bottles. Cut out **BITS OF BLACK AND WHITE PAPER** for the eyes.

6 Cut ears out of **SHINY PAPER** and stick them onto the edge of the bottle. Do you see a donkey in front of you?

7 To give the donkey its mane, glue **THIN COLOURED PAPER** onto the bottle's side.

8 Don't forget a tail!

To move

Push your hand through the bottle and wiggle the donkey up and down.

Twin Heads

Sometimes, two heads are better than one.

 +

 +

 +

To make

1 Take **TWO SAME-SIZED CARDBOARD BOXES** and cut them to make them squares (or any shape you like). Wrap them in **COLOURED PAPER**.

2 Take a third **CARDBOARD BOX** and make two slits on its top end, on both sides. Slide the first two boxes through these slits till they sit firm. Your twin heads are ready.

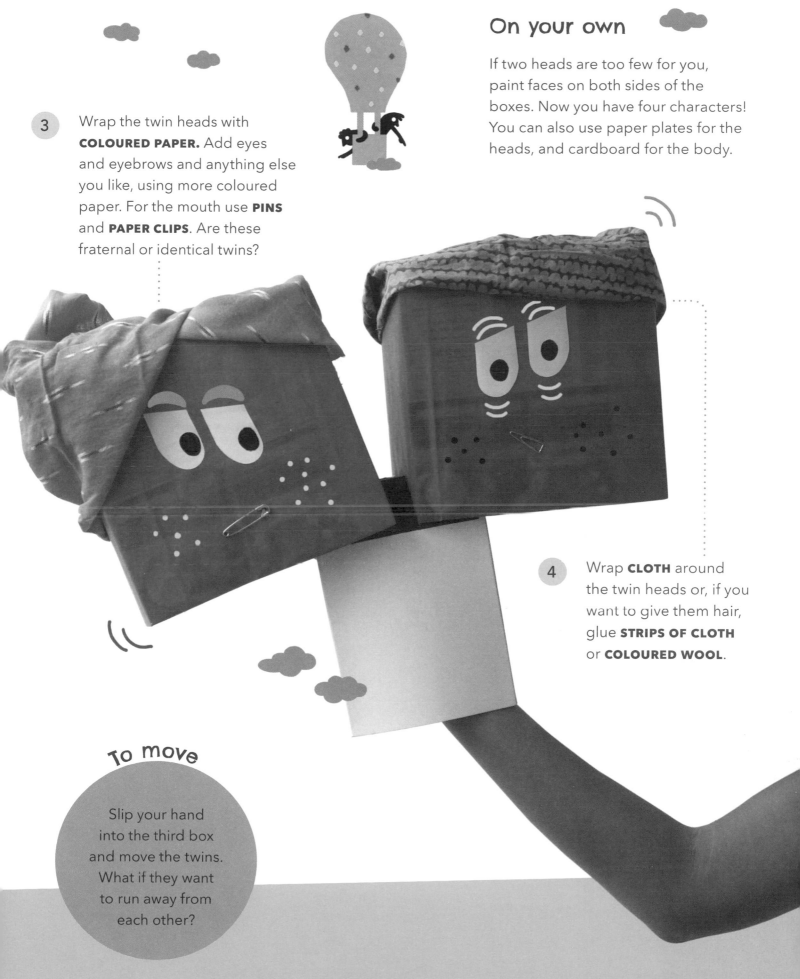

3 Wrap the twin heads with **COLOURED PAPER.** Add eyes and eyebrows and anything else you like, using more coloured paper. For the mouth use **PINS** and **PAPER CLIPS**. Are these fraternal or identical twins?

On your own

If two heads are too few for you, paint faces on both sides of the boxes. Now you have four characters! You can also use paper plates for the heads, and cardboard for the body.

4 Wrap **CLOTH** around the twin heads or, if you want to give them hair, glue **STRIPS OF CLOTH** or **COLOURED WOOL**.

To move

Slip your hand into the third box and move the twins. What if they want to run away from each other?

39

Singing Saint

Draped in saffron robes, this ordinary roll ended up as a saint, singing mournful songs.

To make

1. Take a **TOILET PAPER ROLL** or any other **CARDBOARD ROLL** that you can turn into a body.

2. Take a **NEWSPAPER SHEET** and roll it diagonally till you have a tight newspaper stick.

3. In the cardboard roll, make two holes and insert the newspaper stick through one hole and out of the other. You can bend the stick upwards, if you like.

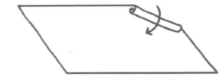

4 Wrap a **BALL** with **CLOTH** to make the head. Glue it to the top of the cardboard roll.

5 Glue long strands of **WOOL** or **COLOURED THREAD** to the ball. And watch your Saint come alive.

6 Drape the saint in suitably coloured **CLOTH**.

On your own

Try making other saintly figures out of different materials: for the head, try stiff dough or even clay. How about using bamboo for the body? Try making ordinary people too.

To move

Put your hand under the cloth and hold the roll with your thumb and forefinger placed on the newspaper sticks. Press the newspaper sticks to move them with true devotion!

Witch

Under all that mysterious paint and strange decorations, this Witch is made of paper. So does she practise 'spell'ing on herself?

To make

1   Make a cone out of **NEWSPAPER**, and glue the edges firmly. This is for the face.

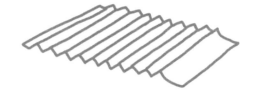

2   Take another piece of newspaper, and fold it into a fan..........

3   Staple this fan at one end so that it opens out like a pleated skirt..........

4   Glue the stapled end of the fan inside the open end of the cone. The skirt is all done now.

5 Colour, draw and decorate the newspaper cone till it looks mysterious enough.

6 For the hair, glue **COLOURED WOOL** onto the tip of the cone. **THIN STRIPS OF COLOURED PAPER** or **COTTON** or **JUTE** should do as well.

7 Cut a small slit for the mouth. Pop your thumb through the slit and the Witch is ready to chant spells!

On your own

Try making a wizard instead of a witch. How about a ballet dancer?

To move

Insert your hand into the cone and make the Witch cast spells on all your friends.

Mr Coco

Though made from a tough coconut sheath, Mr Coco is a gentle sort.

To make

1. Look around for a **COCONUT SHEATH** that you can turn into a face. If you cannot find a coconut sheath, try other **DRIED BARK**. You can also use **CARDBOARD** cut to shape.

2. Use cut-out bits of **PAPER** or **MARKERS** to create eyes and mouth.

3. Use **PIECES OF COCONUT FIBRE** or **ROPE** for eyebrows, moustache, beard and hair.

MR

MS

MS

MR

On your own

▶ Find more coconut ▶ sheaths and create a set of companions for Mr Coco. ▶

4 Tie a piece of rope around the sheath. Mr Coco is ready to move out into the world!

To move it

Insert your hand behind the rope to move Mr Coco. Or just hold the rope and move him around.

ROD PUPPETS

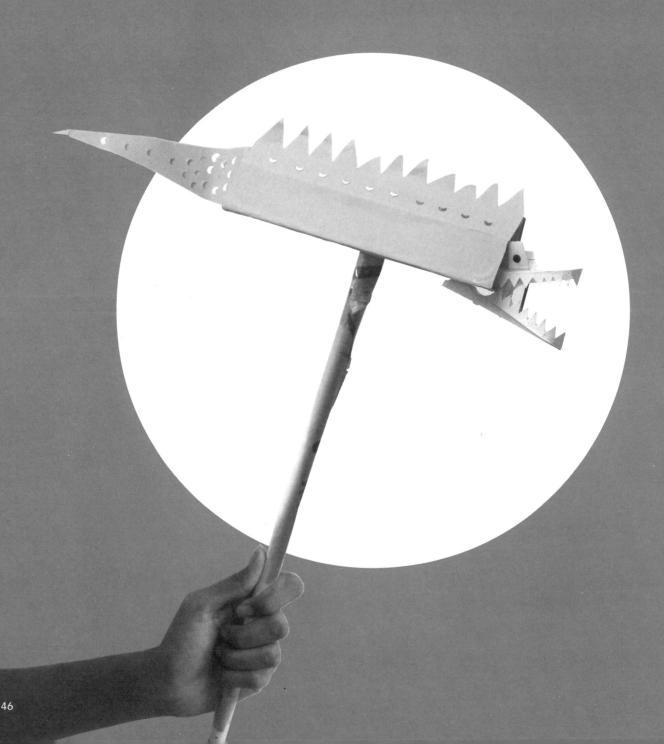

How do they work?

As its name suggests, a rod puppet comes with a stick that is usually attached to the puppet's head. The stick is the central control rod, which is used to move the puppet.

What is special about rod puppets?

Rod puppets can be large or small. Some can be so tiny that you can handle them above a table top. Others can be as big as the puppeteers themselves, or even bigger.

What did we do?

We made our rod puppets out of cloth, cardboard cartons, paper, socks, odds and ends such as clothes hangers, balls, shuttlecocks, bats... Most importantly, we had to devise good control rods — we made newspaper sticks for this purpose.

Jumbo

To make

1 Look for a **COCONUT SHEATH**. If you don't find one, an odd-sized piece of **THICK CARDBOARD** will do for a face.

A coconut sheath is tough and sometimes ambitious. This one aspired to be an elephant.

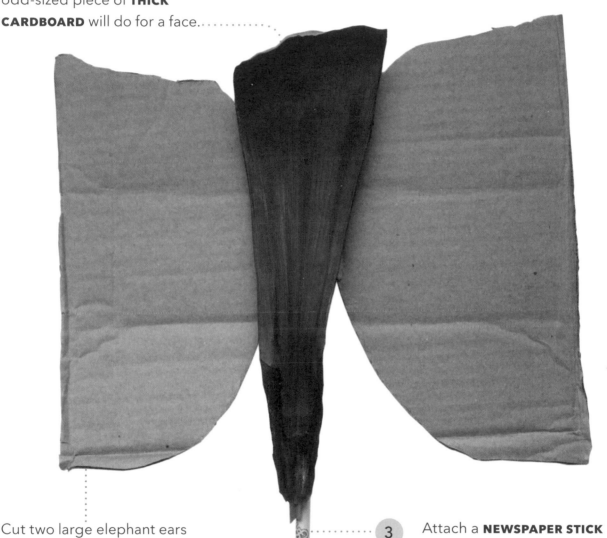

2 Cut two large elephant ears out of **CARDBOARD** and glue them to the sheath.

3 Attach a **NEWSPAPER STICK** to the back of the sheath. This is the central rod.

4 Wrap the cardboard ears in bright **CLOTH**. Glue them onto the back of the sheath a little loosely, so that they can flap back and forth.

5 Use bits of **PAPER** to stick on eyes or draw them using **MARKERS**. Your Jumbo is ready for his morning walk.

On your own

Decorate the elephant's trunk with little drawings. Or give him a cap and other fashion accessories.

6 Roll **PAPER** to make elephant tusks and glue them on. You could also make them from **CARDBOARD** or **THERMOCOL**.

To move

Hold Jumbo up using the central rod. Move the rod so that his ears flap back and forth.

Bat Brat

Here's a sports star with attitude!

To make

1 See if you can get hold of a discarded **TABLE TENNIS BAT** or **TENNIS RACQUET**. These make for interesting faces.

2 Tie **PIECES OF SCRAP CLOTH** to the bat to make thick strands of hair. Cut out **PIECES OF COLOURED PAPER** for eyes, mouth and other features.

3 Accessorise this emerging star with some fashionable **GOGGLES**.

4 Wrap **CLOTH** around the neck of the bat and tie it firmly.

On your own

Try making other batty characters: A priest? A dancer? A guitarist? An astronaut?

To move

Hold up the Bat-handle and watch her wow the audience.

Startled Pig

This pig grew out of a cardboard box and a plastic container. He looks pretty surprised about it.

To make

1. Take a **CARDBOARD BOX** that is thick and sturdy. You can turn this into a face in no time.

2. Cut a circular hole in the cardboard box. Use a **ROUND PLASTIC JAR** or **CONTAINER** to mark out the circle before you cut it. This is for the nose or snout.

3. Make two holes at the base of the box and insert **TWO NEWSPAPER STICKS** through them.

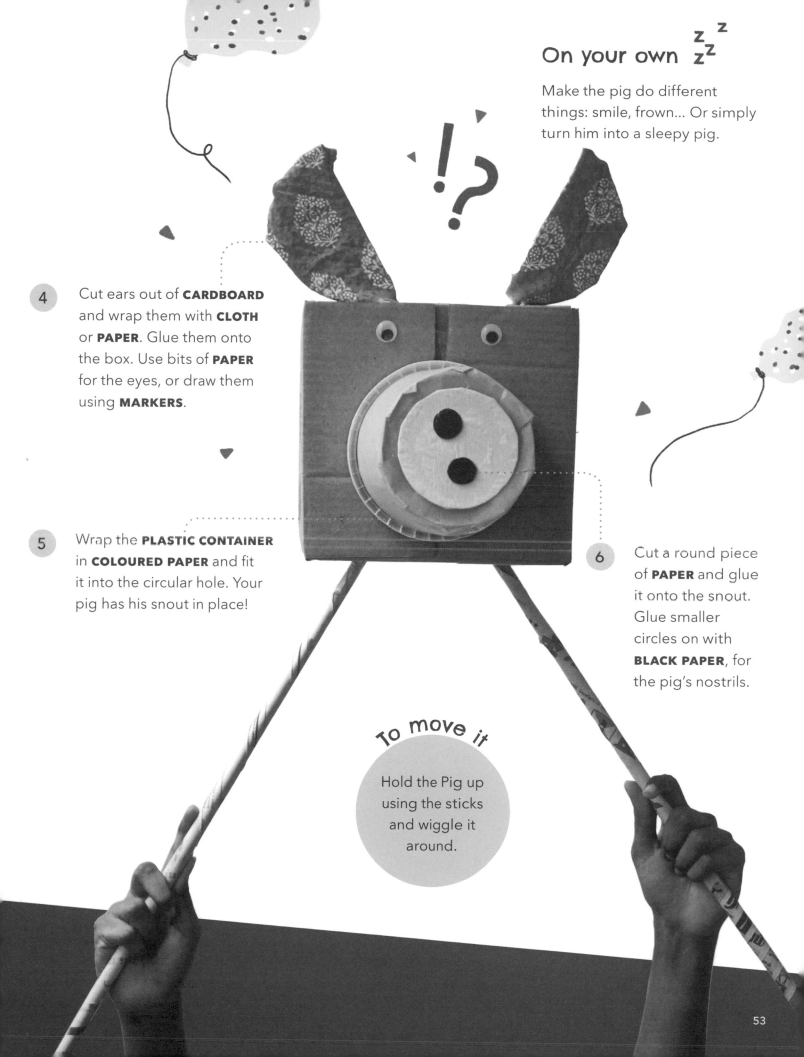

Make the pig do different things: smile, frown... Or simply turn him into a sleepy pig.

4 Cut ears out of **CARDBOARD** and wrap them with **CLOTH** or **PAPER**. Glue them onto the box. Use bits of **PAPER** for the eyes, or draw them using **MARKERS**.

5 Wrap the **PLASTIC CONTAINER** in **COLOURED PAPER** and fit it into the circular hole. Your pig has his snout in place!

6 Cut a round piece of **PAPER** and glue it onto the snout. Glue smaller circles on with **BLACK PAPER**, for the pig's nostrils.

To move it

Hold the Pig up using the sticks and wiggle it around.

53

Toothy 'Gator

This alligator was made from a toothpaste carton. Is that why he has such sharp teeth?

To make

1 Find a **TOOTHPASTE CARTON**. Crease it in such a way that you get this triangular shape. All you need to do now is turn it into an alligator.

2 Make a hole in the base of the carton and insert a **NEWSPAPER STICK**.......

3 Fasten a **CLOTHES CLIP** ············· onto the bottom flap at the end of the carton. That should make for a fine pair of jaws.

4 Cut out bits of **PAPER** for eyes and teeth and glue them onto the plastic clip. Your alligator is ready to snap at the world!

5 Cut two long **STRIPS OF PAPER**. Along one of the long edges cut out a jagged edge. Glue the strips, one on each side of the toothpaste box. Let the strips be longer than the body, so that they extend to form the tail.

6 Stick bits of **SHINY PAPER** onto the paper strips to give the alligator its scales.

To move

Hold up the 'Gator with the newspaper stick and make him glide along the water.

55

Man...

A simple man who does not want much except to share the world with birds and beasts.

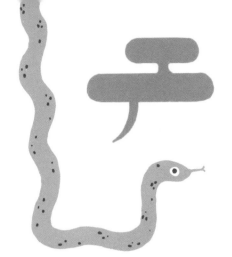

To make

1 Cut out a circle from a piece of **CARDBOARD**. This should do for a head and face.

2 Make two **NEWSPAPER STICKS** and create a cross by laying one on another. Use **THREAD** or **TAPE** to secure the joint tight.

3 Glue the **CARDBOARD** to the top end of the vertical stick.

4 Draw or stick features made out of bits of **PAPER** onto the circular cardboard. Attach a **CLOTH** cap or make one out of **COLOURED PAPER** and glue it on.

5 Cut hands out of **PAPER** and glue them to the ends of both sticks.

6 Drape **CLOTH** over the horizontal stick, and your simple Man is ready for the day's business.

To move it

Hold up the Man by the vertical stick and jiggle him to make him dance.

On your own

Give the simple Man funky accessories.

...and Friend

While the man stayed simple, his friend turned out to be really quirky.

To make

1 Tie **TWO NEWSPAPER STICKS** to form a cross.

2 Stuff an **OLD SOCK** with **STRIPS OF CLOTH** or anything else you can find, even paper or cotton. Fit the stuffed sock over the vertical stick of the newspaper cross. Now you have a head to work with.

3   Glue on **BOTTLE CAPS** for eyes. Use **COLOURED PAPER** for the mouth or other features that you wish to add. Knot the upper end of the sock into a bow and you will see a rather interesting person come to life.

On your own

Name the Friend.

4   Drape **BRIGHT PRINTED CLOTH** over the cross for a shirt. Add some jewellery if you like.

5   To make the hands, tie **STRIPS OF CLOTH** around the two ends of the horizontal stick.

To move

Hold up the Friend by the vertical stick and have him beckon the Man.

59

Prima Donna

Fancy clothes and jewellery converted a small, plain coconut into a glamorous performer. Could this be the beginning of a great singing and dancing career?

To make

1 To make a small, elegant head, look for a **SMALL COCONUT**, with twigs attached. If not, settle for an elongated **POTATO** or **BALL**.

2 Make a hole on one side of the coconut and push a **PENCIL** into it. This takes time and is hard, so do it carefully and slowly.

3 Take a **CARDBOARD SOAP BOX** and make holes on all four sides. Stick the other end of the pencil into the top hole. Now, the coconut has a body.

4 Push a **NEWSPAPER STICK** into the bottom hole.

5 Push another newspaper stick through the side holes such that its two ends stretch out in a horizontal fashion.

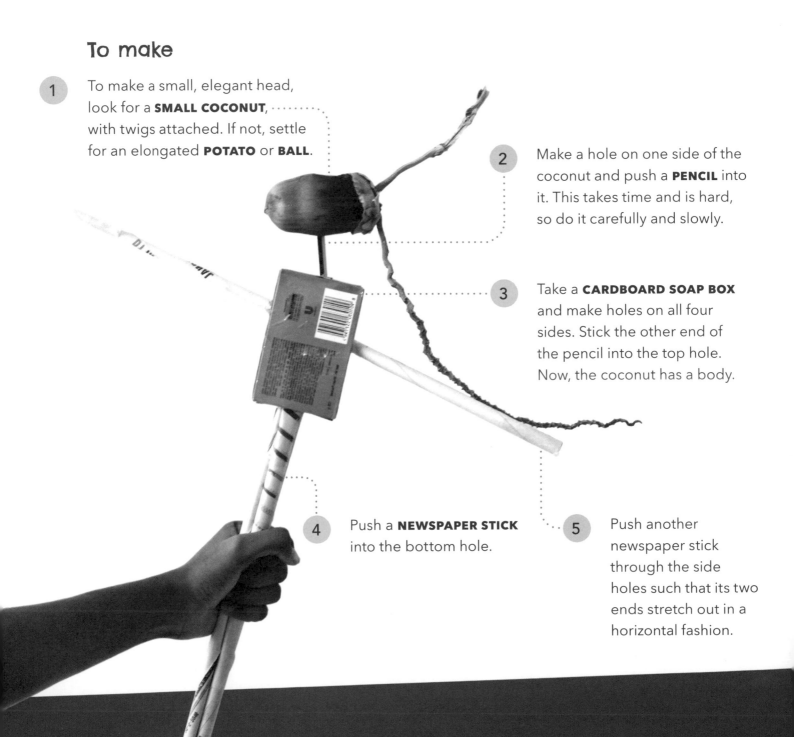

On your own

All singers need not be glamorous nuts. What about a Potato-Head Pop Star or a Rubber-Ball Rapper? You could use carrot slices for earrings and make a necklace of peanut shells. Cut onion rings for bangles. They'll also do for perfume!

6   Roll **PATTERNED PAPER** to make two cylinders. Slide these over the two ends of the horizontal newspaper stick. Make hands and glue them to the arms. Don't forget to cut out bits of **PAPER** for the eyes.

7   Drape the puppet in **COLOURFUL CLOTH** and add jewellery of your choice. Decorate the twig-hair with ribbons. Now you have a Prima Donna all set to conquer the music world.

To move

Hold the puppet up by the main rod. If your puppet has a braid, use it to move the head around.

Hanger-on

What would you normally do with a hanger? Hang clothes, of course! That is exactly what we did, and came up with this obliging Hanger-on.

To make

1 For the head, wrap a **CARDBOARD BOX** or **PAPER PLATE** with **NEWSPAPER** and fix it to the hook of a **CLOTHES HANGER**.

2 Attach the clothes hanger to **TWO NEWSPAPER STICKS** using a piece of **STRING** or **CLOTH**. Your main control rod is now in place.

3 Take another **CARDBOARD BOX**. Make a hole on top and insert the newspaper stick below the hanger.

4 Make two arms from **ROLLED STIFF PAPER** and tie them onto the ends of the hanger.

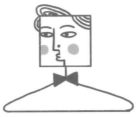

The Hanger-on is anxious.
Where is the Boss?
Make the Boss!

5 Make a face by painting on the newspaper or adding features, using **PIECES OF PAPER**.

6 Put an **OLD T-SHIRT** over the hanger.

7 Cut out hands from **PAPER** and glue them to the arms.

8 Attach a **NEWSPAPER STICK** to one of the arms to move it. Make sure you know if the Hanger-on is a left-hander or a right-hander!

To move

Hold the puppet up using the main rod. Use the other stick to move his arm. Watch out! The Hanger-on wants to hang on to your every word and praise you!

Tiffin Time

Here is a cook-cum-waiter-cum-dinner-gong. When the food is ready, she goes...

To make

1 Take a **LADLE**. Stick bits of **PAPER** to its cup to make features. Your ladle could remain bald or you might want to add a braid, using **STRIPS OF WOOL**. You could also paint on hair.

dong! dong! dong! dong! dong!

2 Tie a **NEWSPAPER STICK** to the ladle using **THREAD** or **TAPE** to form a cross. We wrapped the stick with cloth for the cook's sleeves.

3 Bend the stick on both sides at an angle.

On your own

You can cook up many strange characters if you look around your kitchen. It might be a good idea to ask permission before you help yourself.

4 Wrap **CLOTH** over the stick and the handle of the ladle. Attach a **SMALL SPOON** to one arm and a **SMALL PLATE** to the other using **TAPE**.

dong! dong! dong!

5 Tape or glue a **STICK** behind the plate, to fix your control rod.

To move

Hold up the puppet and move its head using the stem of the ladle. Move the arm, using the control rod. When it is tiffin time, the cook gets all excited and threatens to strike her head!

Hopping Hoopoe

This hoopoe won't stop hopping and showing off, strutting about with his neck darting backwards and forwards.

To make

1. Find a **PAPER PLATE**. Or cut a circle out of a piece of **CARDBOARD**. Ready to make a bird?

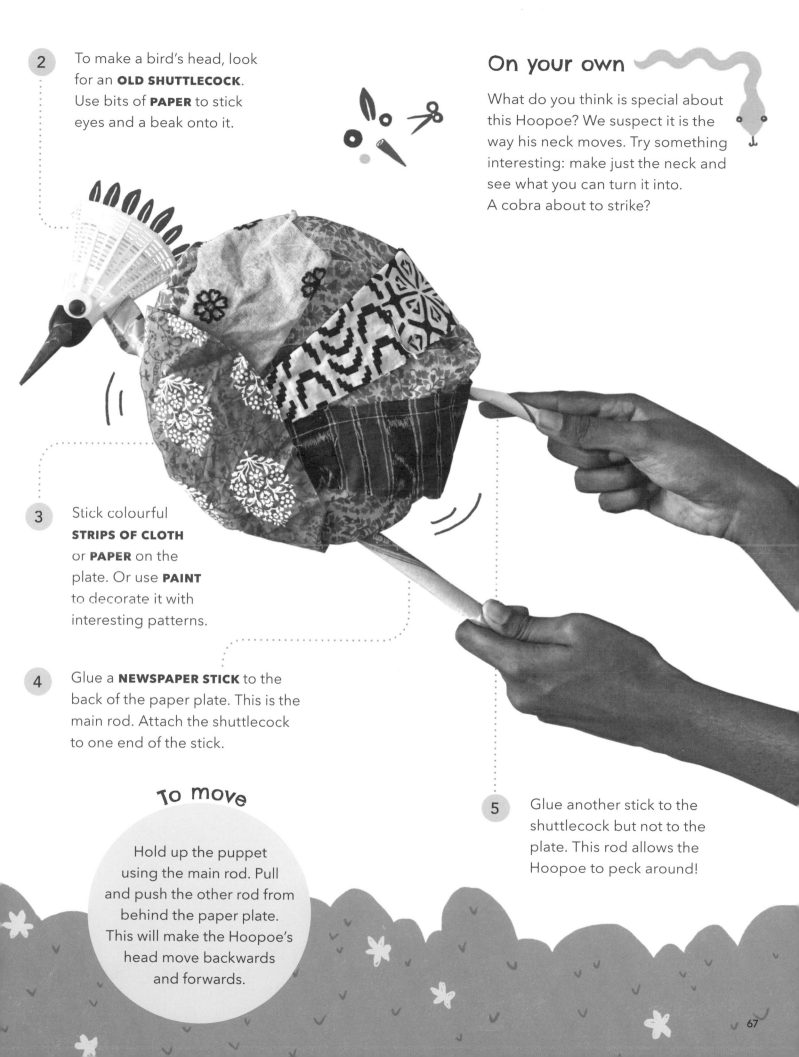

2 To make a bird's head, look for an **OLD SHUTTLECOCK**. Use bits of **PAPER** to stick eyes and a beak onto it.

On your own

What do you think is special about this Hoopoe? We suspect it is the way his neck moves. Try something interesting: make just the neck and see what you can turn it into. A cobra about to strike?

3 Stick colourful **STRIPS OF CLOTH** or **PAPER** on the plate. Or use **PAINT** to decorate it with interesting patterns.

4 Glue a **NEWSPAPER STICK** to the back of the paper plate. This is the main rod. Attach the shuttlecock to one end of the stick.

To move

Hold up the puppet using the main rod. Pull and push the other rod from behind the paper plate. This will make the Hoopoe's head move backwards and forwards.

5 Glue another stick to the shuttlecock but not to the plate. This rod allows the Hoopoe to peck around!

Dracula

Dracula has thrown a great party but no one has dared to turn up. Fang goodness!

To make

1 Find a **COCONUT LEAF SHEATH**. If you can't, use a piece of cardboard.

2 Tie brightly coloured **CLOTH** around the bottom half of the sheath. Cut out hands from **PAPER** and stick them to the cloth on both sides.

3 Fold a **NEWSPAPER STICK** in half to make a V-shape. Attach the ends of the V-shaped stick to each of the hands.

You might want to make a toothy happy monster, instead of Dracula. Use a different shape for the head!

4 Cut out bits of **BLACK AND WHITE PAPER** for features and stick them onto the top part of the sheath.

To move

Hold up the puppet using the bottom end of the coconut sheath and move its arms with the newspaper stick. This Dracula does not wait for moonlight, he can be up and about during the day!

Bat Boy

Do not confuse this mild-mannered person with Batman.

To make

1 Look for an **OLD BADMINTON** or **TENNIS RACQUET.**

2 Cover one side of the racquet with **PAPER** and notice how the racquet has a face now.

Wholesome Nutrition And Delicious Taste!

3 Take a **CARDBOARD BOX** and make a hole at the top and bottom. Slide the racquet handle through the box. Bat-face has a box-body!

4 Use strands of **WOOL** for hair.

5 Cut features out of **PAPER** and stick them on.

6 Drape **CLOTH** over the box and pin it in place.

7 Bat Boy loves to show off his medals. Make him one!

8 Tie a **PLASTIC BAT** to the cloth on one side. Attach a **NEWSPAPER STICK** to the smaller bat. This will help you move the puppet.

To move

Hold the puppet up using the handle of the racquet and move the hand with the newspaper rod.

71

SHADOW PUPPETS

How do they work?

A shadow puppet is always part of a performance. It is placed behind a white screen and the audience sits on the other side. The puppet is lit by a strong light from behind the screen, and when it is held up or moves, its shadow falls on the screen.

Traditionally in India, a shadow puppet is made of leather. Different parts of the puppet are made separately. These are loosely jointed, and moved using thin horizontal rods or wires.

Shadow puppets can be plain or they can have intricate designs cut into them. When the light shines through the cut-out parts, interesting patterns appear on the screen.

What is special about shadow puppets?

Because of the play of light, shadow puppets have a magical and dramatic quality. Unexpected things, like twigs, branches and leaves, can make interesting shadows. You can even create shadows using only your hands!

What did we do?

Instead of leather we used stiff cardboard, and tied the joints with thread. We cut designs onto the cardboard and pasted coloured cellophane paper over the cut-out parts for the light to filter through.

To hold the puppets up, we used long, thin sticks instead of newspaper sticks, so that they were not so visible. We also set up a screen. We made sure that it was lit from behind, and then shut the windows and doors and had our own puppet shows.

Moo-dy Cow

We made a cow but she wouldn't make a sound. She seemed the strong, silent type.

To make

1 Take a sheet of **BLACK PAPER** or a piece of **CARDBOARD**. Draw the head and body of the cow onto the sheet. Cut these out separately.

2 Make a hole for the eye. Draw patterns and shapes on the cow's body. Cut these out so that the light can shine through. Use bits of **COLOURED CELLOPHANE PAPER** to cover the cut-out parts. Don't forget to cover the eye!

3 Join the cow's head and body using **STRING**. Make sure that they overlap slightly and are loosely jointed so that movement is easy.

4 Glue a **TALL STICK** to the cow's body. This is the main rod. Attach another to its head.

74

Turn the cow into a reindeer. Is she as strong and silent as the cow?

To move

Hold the cow up by the main rod, and move the other rod upwards. Does your cow moo? If she does not, you might have to make the sound yourself.

Dancing Peacock

People say peacocks dance when it is about to rain. But this one takes no notice of the weather.

To make

1 Draw the outline of a peacock on a piece of **THICK BLACK PAPER.** Cut the body and head out separately. For the tail, draw each feather singly and cut each one of them out.

2 Cut out eyes on the head and other designs on the body and tail. Make sure you don't have too many designs – the peacock might flop and fall down.

3 Glue bits of **COLOURED CELLOPHANE PAPER** over the cut out areas.

4 Join the two parts – body and tail – with a slight overlap using **STRING.**

5 Glue one **STICK** to the body and the other to the tail.

On your own

Let your Peacock really get into the dancing mood! Make it 'rain' by sprinkling down pieces of paper or grains of rice from behind the screen.

To move

Hold up the Peacock using the main body rod, and move the other one to make it dance. Keep an umbrella handy just in case it begins to rain.

Creepers & Crawlers

How about a set of creepy crawly characters for your performance?

To make

(1) Draw the outlines of real and imaginary insects on a piece of **THICK BLACK PAPER**, and cut them out.

(2) Use a **PAPER PUNCH** to make holes on the cut-out insects. You can decorate the creatures in other ways as well. Work carefully with a **CUTTER.**

(3) Glue **PIECES OF COLOURED CELLOPHANE PAPER** over the holes. You can even leave some blank!

(4) Glue a **STICK** behind each of the insects.

On your own

The creatures are ready to rush around, but where is the garden?
Cut plants and flowers out of black paper, or experiment with objects that create forest-like shadows against the screen.

To move

Since these insects don't have joints, you can only move them from one end of the screen to the other, holding them by the sticks.

Snake in the Grass

A glittery slithery serpent, ready to crawl around in the grass.

To make

1 Draw the outline of a snake's head and long narrow rectangles for its body on a piece of **THICK BLACK PAPER**. Cut these out.

2 Make holes and patterns on the head and body of the snake, using a **CUTTER**. Don't forget the eyes.

3 Glue bits of **COLOURED CELLOPHANE PAPER** over the holes.

On your own

The grass! Don't forget to make the grass!

4 Punch holes at both ends of each rectangle and tie the rectangles together with **STRING**. The different pieces must overlap slightly. Join the head and the body pieces similarly, but knot the string tight in this case.

5 Attach **STICKS** to alternate pieces using **TAPE**.

To move

To operate the puppet, hold it up with the sticks and move them up and down. This will make the Snake curve and slither. It takes more than one person to move this Snake!

Cardboardus Cellophanum

This is a giant polka-dotted-pink-and-green-pigeon-moth butterfly.

Zoological name: Cardboardus Cellophanum

To make

1. Draw the outline of a butterfly on a piece of **THICK BLACK PAPER.**

2. Cut out decorative holes and patterns in the body and wings.

3. Glue **PIECES OF COLOURED CELLOPHANE PAPER** over the holes and patterns.

4. Glue a **STICK** to each wing of the butterfly so you can make it flap.

On your own

Get this rather seriously named butterfly to flap and dance! Hint: you might need to make the puppet in three parts.

To move

Move the two rods to make the flutterby butterfly – or should that be the other way round?

Crow & Nest

This crow's nest is ready much before the others. So she can't stop crowing about it!

To make

1. Draw the outline of a flying crow on **THICK BLACK PAPER.**

2. Cut out slits for feathers with a **CUTTER** and punch a hole for the eye.

3. Attach a **STICK** near the tail.

4. To make the nest, gather a **BUNCH OF STICKS** and tie them in the middle with **STRING.**

5. Cut out two eggs from **BLACK PAPER** and stick them on the nest.

6. Attach a **STICK** at the bottom to move the nest with.

On your own

Maybe some of the eggs have hatched? Add baby crows!

To move

Hold up the Crow with the main stick and make it fly around. Make sure the nest stays still.

Giant Giraffe

This is a very tall giraffe... is that because of his neck or legs?

To make

1. Draw the outline of a giraffe in two parts on a sheet of **CARDBOARD**: the body, legs and tail form one unit, while the head and neck form the other. If the neck flops, attach a **NEWSPAPER STICK** behind it to hold it up.

2. Cut out spots along the neck and body and cover them with bits of **COLOURED CELLOPHANE PAPER.**

3. Overlap the two parts slightly, and join them using **STRING.**

4. Attach two **STURDY STICKS** using **TAPE** — one to the body of the giraffe, and the other to the neck.

On your own

A tall elephant?
A tall and fat elephant?

To move

Hold the Giraffe up with the main stick for the body and use the other stick to move its long and elegant neck.

STRING PUPPETS

How do they work?

A string puppet has a body with moveable parts controlled by strings. To stop the puppet from swinging about, there is also a main string which the puppeteer needs to hold firmly.

The strings of the puppet are tied to a cross-shaped piece of wood, called the control. If you're a skilled puppeteer, you can move all the different parts of the puppet just by handling the control. String puppets are also called marionettes.

What is special about string puppets?

When the strings are almost invisible, the puppets look as if they are moving by themselves, magically. They can be really lifelike.

What did we do?

String puppets are the hardest kind of puppets to make and move. We had to keep one thing in mind: that the puppets could move easily. So, we had to ensure that clothing didn't come in the way, and that the joints held firmly.

For the control cross, we used newspaper sticks. But it was not always easy to work the strings. We had to learn to be patient and skillful. Ultimately, we found that the puppets with the simplest mechanisms and which required the least number of strings worked best for us.

Flower Power

Put a pot of flowers on an ordinary girl and give her extra powers.

To make

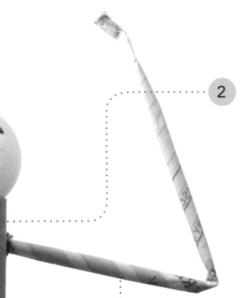

1 Draw a face on a **PLASTIC BALL** with a **MARKER.** This is the head...

2 Glue the ball to the top of a **CARDBOARD ROLL.** This is the body of your puppet.

3 Make two holes on either side of the roll. Take a **NEWSPAPER STICK** and insert a **LONG STRING** through it. Pass the newspaper stick through the roll. The puppet has her arms in place now.

4 Tie the ends of the string to a **NEWSPAPER CROSS**.

On your own

Instead of a flower girl with flower power, you could make a leaf girl or a fruit girl...

5 Use **STRIPS OF CLOTH** or **PAPER** for hair. Stick a **PAPER CUP** on top of the head and decorate it with **FLOWERS** and **LEAVES**. Make a bouquet for the flower girl to hold.

6 Attach a **STRING** to the cup and tie it to the middle of the cross. The control has three strings attached to it now: one from the head, and the other two from the arms of the puppet.

7 Stick a piece of **COLOURED PAPER** around the cardboard roll to make a shirt.

8 Gather some paper into pleats, and glue it onto the lower end of the cardboard roll. If you like, give her a belt using a brightly coloured **STRIP OF CLOTH**.

To move

Hold the puppet up using the string tied to the cup. Move the other two strings to get the flower girl to dance and sell flowers.

Pop Star

This character likes to get a completely new look for every show. Perhaps she ought to wear only disposable clothes!

To make

1 Turn a **PAPER CUP** upside down. Using **TAPE**, attach a **NEWSPAPER STICK** to it.

2 Slide a **TOILET PAPER ROLL** up the newspaper stick. Glue it to the upper part of the stick, just below the paper cup.

3 Take another **NEWSPAPER STICK** and insert a **LONG STRING** through it. The string ought to be long enough to extend beyond both ends of the newspaper stick.

4 Make two holes on the sides of the toilet paper roll and push the second newspaper stick with the string through it. Your Pop Star is all set to get her look for the day.

On your own

For her forthcoming show, the Pop Star needs a new and improved head. Help her find one.

5 Make a **NEWSPAPER CROSS**. Attach the ends of the string from the horizontal newspaper stick to two ends of the cross. Run a **STRING** from the cup to the centre of the cross.

6 Use a **MARKER** to draw eyes, eyebrows and a mouth onto the paper cup. Wrap some **RIBBON** over cardboard roll. This should do for a blouse.

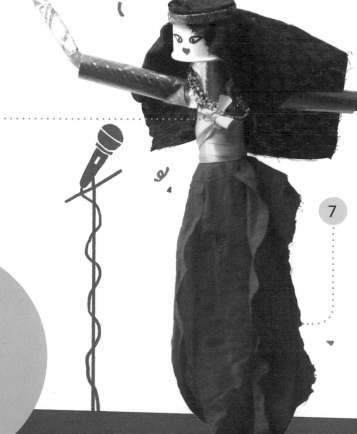

7 Take a piece of **CLOTH** and gather it into pleats. Glue it to the lower end of the roll. If you like, give the emerging star a headscarf.

To move it

Tie the other ends of the strings to the newspaper cross. The Pop Star is ready for the lights!

✳ Coco ✳ Cliperella

Made of coconut shell and paper clips, this lady has found an ideal job with a coconut exporter, clipping papers left and right.

To make

1 Find a **COCONUT SHELL**. Now you have a basic face to work with. Create the features using a **MARKER** or bits of **PAPER**.

2 Fix a **NEWSPAPER STICK** vertically to the base of the coconut shell, or behind it.

3 Slide a **TOILET PAPER ROLL** over the stick and tape it in place. This is the body. To give the puppet a blouse, wrap the roll in **COLOURED PAPER**.

4 Make two holes on the sides of the roll and pass a **LONG STRING** through. Make two tubes out of **BLACK PAPER** and slide these over the string on either side of the roll. . . . .

5 Two **BIG PAPER CLIPS** make the hands. Attach the paper clips – or anything else you like – to the black tubes with string. . . . .

6 Tie a string to each of these clips and tie these strings to a **NEWSPAPER CROSS**. Attach another string from the top of the head to the centre of the cross.

7 Wrap a piece of **CLOTH** around the toilet roll. The puppet's sari is in place now.

On your own

Change the character by dressing her differently. Clip papers on to her hands to make her look official.

8 Give the puppet a braid made of **FAKE HAIR** or **BLACK RIBBONS**.

To move

Use the newspaper stick to move Coco Cliperella and get her clipping!

95

Jazzy Jester

To make

1 Find a **PLASTIC BALL.** Cut out eyes from bits of **COLOURED PAPER** and stick them onto the face or use **PAINT.** Make a conical hat from **PAPER.** You have a fine Jester in the making.

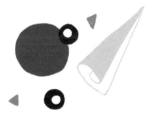

2 Wrap a **SMALL CARDBOARD BOX** with **COLOURED PAPER.** The jazzier the Jester's clothes the better!

3 Make two holes on the sides of the box, at both the top and bottom.

4 Thread one **LONG STRING** through the top holes of the box and another slightly longer string through the bottom holes.

5 Slip **FOUR DRINKING STRAWS** over the strings, at both the top and bottom. These make good hands and legs.

He wouldn't want you to know, but under his fancy costume, this jazzy type is actually made of a juice box and straws.

See what kind of character the Jazzy Jester becomes if you don't paste paper all over him. If you like, you can even cover him up with something else instead, like feathers or cotton.

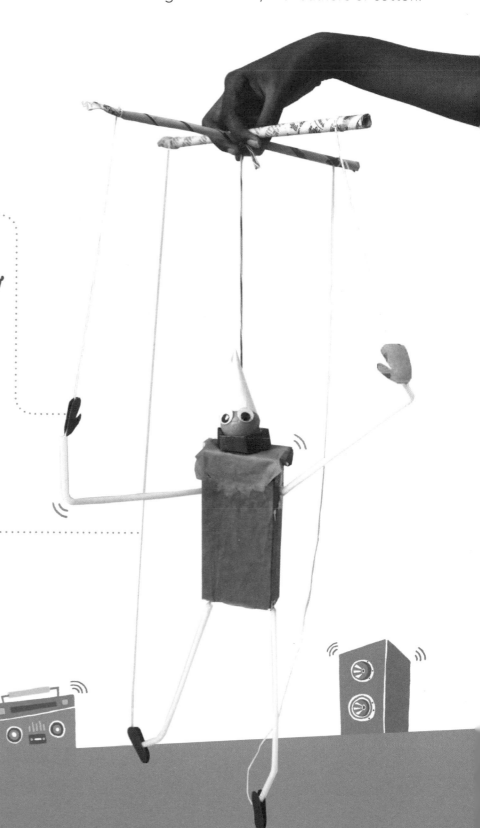

6 Cut out **PAPER** hands and feet and glue them to the strings to keep the straws from slipping through.

7 Make a **NEWSPAPER CROSS.** Attach a **STRING** from the head to the middle of the cross. Next, attach the leg strings to one stick of the cross and the hand strings onto the other. Remember the strings for the legs have to be the longest, the string for the hands slightly shorter, and the string to their head has to be the shortest.

To move

Hold the cross carefully and move the strings that link to the hands and feet of the Jester. Get him to dance to a jazzy tune.

Bouncing Boa

This fellow looks like a snake, but moves like a rabbit. He bounces about merrily instead of slithering silently.

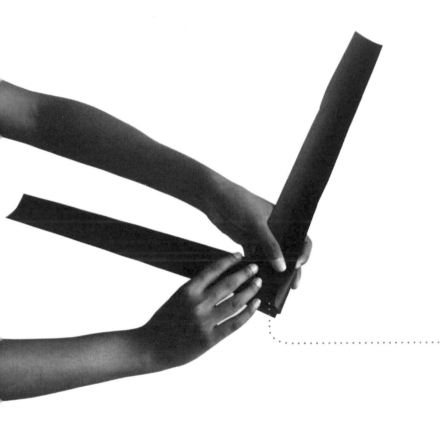

To make

1. Cut **TWO LONG STRIPS OF PAPER** of equal width and length. You could also use **THICK RIBBONS** or **GIFT WRAPPING PAPER** instead. Glue them at right angles to each other.

2. Fold one strip over the other, and then the other one over the first one.

3. Continue folding this way, until you get a long streamer, like a paper decoration. Close the ends by gluing them down so they don't unravel. This is the body of the snake.

On your own ⌇⌇⌇⌇

Make up a story about a snake that cannot, does not and will not slither.

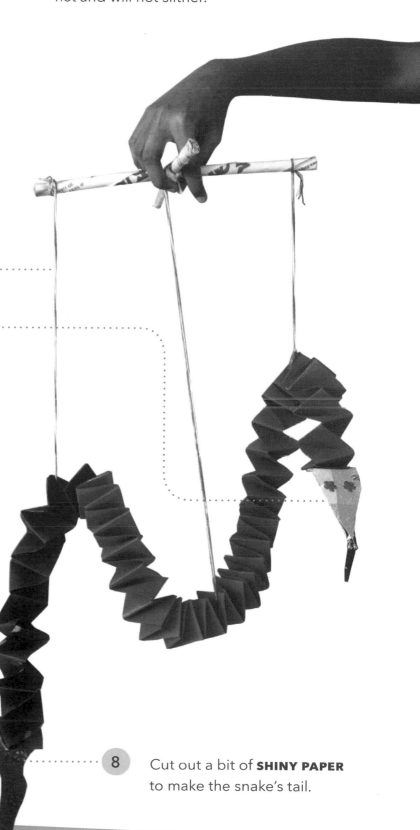

4 Attach **THREE STRINGS** at different places along the snake's body. Tie the other ends of the strings to the newspaper cross, one at the centre and two on either end. Your snake is ready to bounce along.............

5 Cut a piece of **COLOURED PAPER** in the shape of a snake's head. Glue it to one end of the snake-streamer.

6 Cut eyes and a forked tongue out of **PAPER** or anything else you can find. Glue them to the head.

7 Glue one end of the paper streamer to the base of the head.

To move

Hold the puppet up using the control. The Snake will hop along merrily, just like a rabbit.

8 Cut out a bit of **SHINY PAPER** to make the snake's tail.

99

Ms Bald

Remember, bald is beautiful.

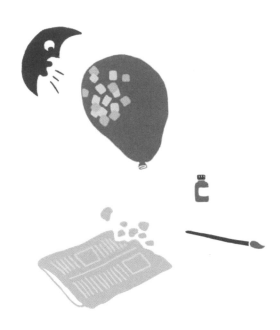

To make

1 Blow a **BALLOON** and secure its mouth tightly with a **STRING**. Glue small **PIECES OF NEWSPAPER** over the balloon, covering it completely. Let it dry overnight and then paint it a bright colour.

2 Wrap some **CARDBOARD** — it can be any shape you like — in **COLOURFUL PAPER**. This forms the top half of the body.

3 Tape or glue a **NEWSPAPER STICK** behind the cardboard.

4 Make two holes on either side of the body and slide **TWO PIECES OF TWISTED WIRE BRAIDED WITH WOOL** through them. Don't forget to twist them into place.

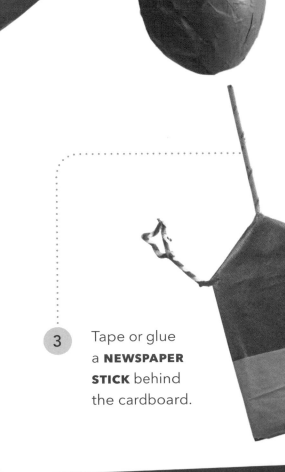

5 Attach the dry balloon head to the newspaper stick. The head and body are now ready.

6 Paint or draw features for Ms Bald. If you like, give her a small bun of hair, made of **CLOTH**.

To move

Hold the puppet up using the control cross, and move her about carefully. She is worried about hitting her head and injuring it.

On your own

How about making Ms Balder and Ms Baldest?

7 Tie long **PIECES OF STRING** to the hands and head. Attach all of them to a **NEWSPAPER CROSS**: the head to the centre and hands to the two sides.

8 Give her fashionable clothes. We made a skirt out of **COLOURFUL WOOL**. Why don't you use **STRIPS OF COLOURFUL PAPER**?!

Jumpy Joker

This funny little fellow hops and jumps obligingly, when you jiggle him about.

To make

1 Find **TWO TIN CANS**, preferably one smaller than the other. Stick the smaller one on top of the bigger one. This is the head and body of the puppet.

2 Wrap strands of **COLOURFUL WOOL** around the cans. You can also use **STRIPS OF PAPER**.

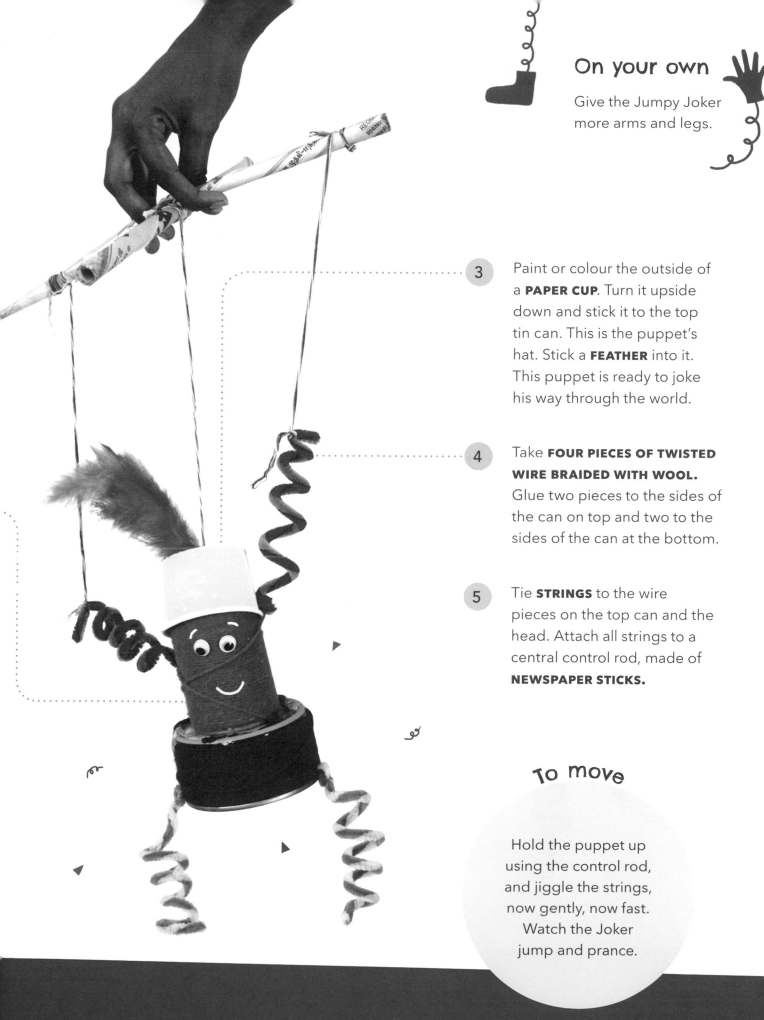

3. Paint or colour the outside of
a **PAPER CUP**. Turn it upside
down and stick it to the top
tin can. This is the puppet's
hat. Stick a **FEATHER** into it.
This puppet is ready to joke
his way through the world.

4. Take **FOUR PIECES OF TWISTED
WIRE BRAIDED WITH WOOL.**
Glue two pieces to the sides of
the can on top and two to the
sides of the can at the bottom.

5. Tie **STRINGS** to the wire
pieces on the top can and the
head. Attach all strings to a
central control rod, made of
NEWSPAPER STICKS.

To move

Hold the puppet up
using the control rod,
and jiggle the strings,
now gently, now fast.
Watch the Joker
jump and prance.

Pentapus

This octopus has only five legs and he's okay with it!

To make

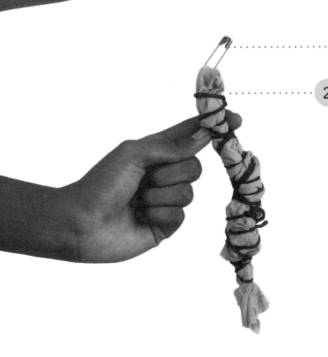

1 Take a large piece of **CLOTH** and stuff it with **SMALLER PIECES OF WASTE CLOTH**. You can also use cotton. Tie it up tightly at the bottom.

2 Find **STRIPS OF CLOTH** in different colours. Roll each of them into a twisted shape. Wrap **WOOL** or **STRING** around each to keep the twist in place.

3 Using **SAFETY PINS**, attach each of the twists to the stuffed piece of cloth — and watch a sea creature with multi-coloured tentacles come to life.

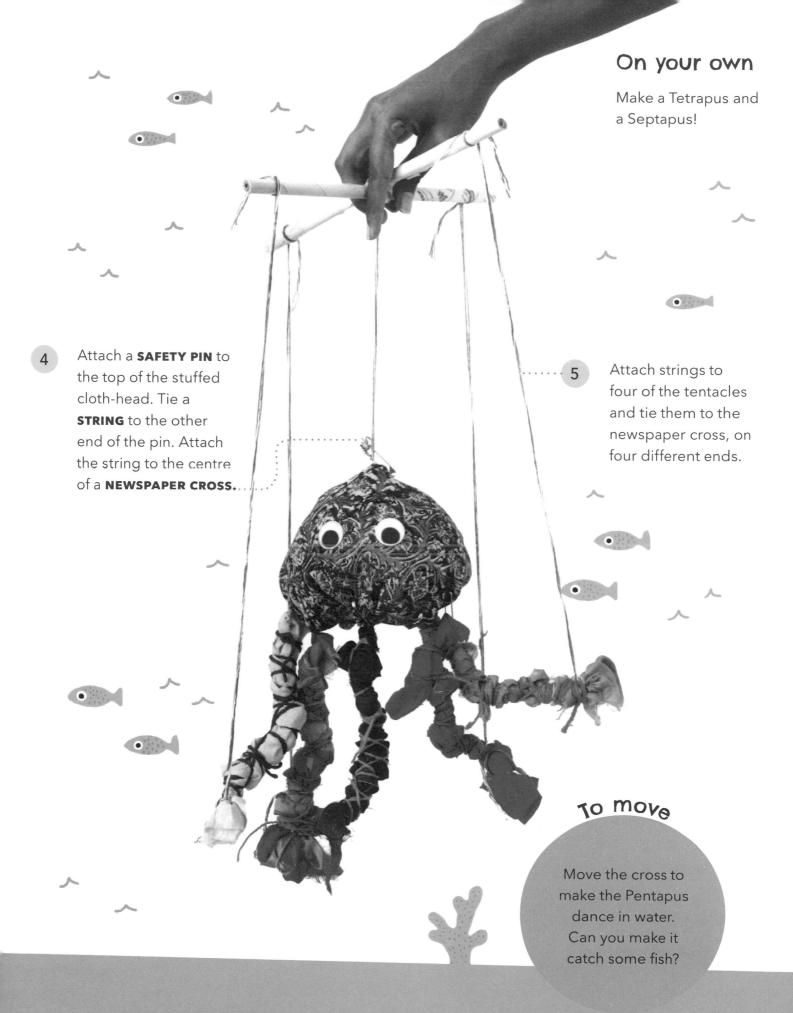

4 Attach a **SAFETY PIN** to the top of the stuffed cloth-head. Tie a **STRING** to the other end of the pin. Attach the string to the centre of a **NEWSPAPER CROSS**.

5 Attach strings to four of the tentacles and tie them to the newspaper cross, on four different ends.

To move

Move the cross to make the Pentapus dance in water. Can you make it catch some fish?

TRADITIONAL PUPPETS

Where did we learn?

Before we started making the puppets in this book, we asked professional puppeteers from different parts of India to teach us how to make puppets. The first thing they showed us were their own traditional puppets, which were beautiful and took a lot of time to create. These puppet masters had been making them for as long as they could remember, but they told us that there are less and less puppeteers now. Puppetry is one of the oldest arts in the world, and people think that puppet theatres began in India and China thousands of years ago, which then spread to other parts of the world. A few of these old ways still exist, but many have died out.

Adapting the old ways

We really admired the beautiful traditional puppets we saw, but there was one thing we knew right away: it would be too hard and take too much time for us to learn to make them. So we decided to just keep the principles of traditional puppetry in mind — because we wanted our puppets to move as easily and effortlessly as traditional puppets did. However, we worked with simple and easily available materials, and came up with our own stories.

Traditional puppeteers

Traditional Indian puppeteers used to make their puppets out of leather, fabric, wood or bamboo. It needed years of training to make these puppets. There are still a few master puppet makers around, but not many. In the old days, puppetry and drama were the most popular forms of entertainment. Everyone knew the old stories very well, so the fun was in the different ways in which they were told. When the puppets were not being used, the puppet master would keep them in his own bedroom. If a puppet became old and could no longer be used, it was never just thrown away. It was taken to a river, and cast into the water, to the chanting of sacred verses.

Kinds of
Traditional Puppets

There is no limit to puppet characters, and each can look very different. But interestingly, as we've seen in this book, there are only four main traditional puppet forms, based on how they work, or are made to move. The four kinds of puppets in this book are based on the four traditional types: hand, rod, shadow and string.

Hand Puppets

Hand puppets have been around for a long time, across the world. Traditionally, the puppeteer sits at a lower level, hidden behind a screen, and pushes the puppet up on the stage. But traditional Indian hand puppeteers sit on the ground with their puppets and can be seen by the audience. The most famous hand puppets in India are from Kerala, which look exactly like traditional dancers.

Rod Puppets

Most traditional rod puppets, like hand puppets, are operated from below the stage, and the puppeteer usually holds up the puppet from below. Rod puppets can be in all sizes: from very large to quite small. The most famous traditional rod puppets are from Indonesia — they are small and beautifully carved out of wood. Their joints are so flexible that puppeteers can make them dance!

Shadow Puppets

Shadow puppetry is said to have originated in China and India. The puppeteer is hidden behind a screen, and his puppets throw magical shadows. There is an interesting Chinese legend about shadow puppetry, where a court magician comforted a king who had lost his wife by creating a shadow puppet resembling the dead queen. The emperor was overjoyed, because he thought the shadow was the spirit of his wife returning.

String Puppets

String puppets are also called marionettes. They are operated from above. In Europe, the tradition of making marionettes is very old. Some of the puppets, carved from wood, look and act like real people on stage. They even have whole operas performed by puppets! You can imagine how many puppeteers, musicians and assistants need to work together, for such a performance. Just keeping the strings of the different puppets from getting entangled must be a difficult job.

Where have they gone?

These days, traditional puppetry shows are quite rare. For one thing, when cinema, television and now online entertainment came along, less and less people went to see puppet shows. People pass time in so many other ways that sadly, most traditional puppeteers can't make a living out of puppetry any more. But this doesn't mean that puppetry as a whole has died out completely. There are new forms these days, and there's something about a live puppet show which is really exciting.

SHOWTIME!

Putting up a puppet show

You might like to hang out with your puppet, alone or with your friends, without actually putting up a performance. But if you do want to have a show starring your puppets, then you have to make preparations.

You will have to think about a whole lot of things: the story script, sound effects, lighting, stage, props and rehearsals. It's just like a regular drama production. But it's not too difficult, and it can be really exciting, if you know how to go about it. To help you avoid the messes and embarrassments we went through while putting up our shows, here are a few tips from us.

Which comes first: the puppet or the script?

If you have already made your puppets, you are saved the trouble of taking this decision. You just have to put them into a story.

If you decide to do the script first, you need to make the right kind of puppet for it. For instance, if your story needs a lot of facial expressions, don't choose shadow puppets.

It's usually better to use only one type of puppet for a performance. Rod and hand puppets can sometimes perform together. But usually, each kind of puppet needs a different kind of stage, and different types of lighting. Mixing them up could cause all sorts of problems.

Making your own story

If you are going to make up your own story, you need to first find out what characters you have on hand.

Move your puppet about, and find out what it can do best. What kind of character does it have? Does it look happy, sad, good, evil, funny? Does it have any peculiar quality? Floppy ears? Big nose? A squint? Does it move in a strange or peculiar way? You could weave in these peculiarities into the story you are going to create.

First come up with a good plot – how it all starts, what happens next, how it ends. All good plots have a 'high point' which makes the story exciting. Once you have a good story, write out a playscript, which should have both the action and dialogue written up. The playscript can either have a lot of action or a lot of words – or a good mixture of both. If your script depends on dialogue, remember that too much talking, without action, might bore your audience.

Write out the script scene by scene. Make sure that there are not too many characters in each scene, otherwise the puppets and the puppeteers will get in each other's way.

Using an existing story

You can use an existing story or modify it to suit the puppets you have. You might have to change a male character into a female one, or vice versa. You can even cut out a few characters and keep the story really simple.

Rehearsals

The more you rehearse, the better your performance will be. Before you begin rehearsals, make sure your script is fully ready. It is always better to work with a definite script. Of course, you can be spontaneous and add lines on the spot. But remember that the others should be able to respond. Decide the exits and entrances on the stage beforehand, so that everyone knows who is going to appear next. Your puppets can come in and go out, just as actors in a play do, or you can have them pop on and off the stage.

As you rehearse, you will find out things that go wrong with each puppet. For example, a puppet's clothes may be coming in the way and restricting its movement. Another one might have a sagging neck, so its head just won't stay up. Make the necessary changes. A few of you who are not part of a scene, can act as the audience, during the rehearsals. You can then give suggestions and comments to improve the show.

The storyboard

Before starting rehearsals, you could make some rough sketches. It helps to plan the performance, because it gives you an idea of how many scenes, sets and props you will need, how many characters there are and what kind of lighting or sound effects will be required. Make a list of the characters and the sets and props needed. Mark the places where lighting is required, and where music and sound effects are to be used. Each person in the group could be responsible for one aspect of the performance. For example, one of you might not want to operate a puppet, and would rather do the music for the play.

Sound effects

All stage performances use sound effects to create atmosphere. They have songs and background music, and sometimes, special sounds that go with the scene. You can choose familiar tunes or songs and put in your own words to suit the story. Try to create special sound effects for rain, thunder, a knock on the door, trees swaying in the wind or footsteps. You can clang pots and pans, bang on table-tops, drag a brush against a plate.

Sets and props

Sets and props provide the background for the performance. The sets show the place where the action is happening. But remember not to overcrowd the stage with too much. You don't want your puppets bumping into chairs and tripping over stools all the time!

Experiment with cardboard cut-outs, paint or coloured paper. Clouds can be made from cotton wool, and fences from matchsticks. You can make three-dimensional sets using match boxes.

Props are objects which the 'actors' can use during the performance. Your puppets can be made to pick up things from the floor, or give things to each other. For example, a hand puppet, such as a dog, can be made to pick up a ball in its mouth.

The stage

The kind of stage needed for a performance depends on the type of puppet you are using:

FOR HAND AND ROD PUPPETS: For puppets operated from below, you can sit or kneel behind a table and hold your puppets above the table-top. You can also turn the table onto its side and sit behind it.

FOR SHADOW PUPPETS: Stretch a dark sheet of cloth over the bottom half of the doorway, and a thin white cloth over the top half. You can crouch behind the dark cloth, so that your shadow does not fall on the screen, and hold your puppets against the white cloth.

FOR STRING PUPPETS: An open doorway can be used for string puppet shows. Cover the lower half of the door with a sheet of cloth, and let the puppets perform in front of it. If you do not wish to be seen by the audience, stretch another sheet of cloth across the top half of the doorway. Remember to leave enough room for your arms, to operate the puppets.

Lighting

Lighting is especially important in a shadow play. The light source should be behind the screen and the puppets. If you are using an open doorway for a stage, natural sunlight can give enough lighting. Another way is to close all doors and windows, except one. The screen can then be placed before the open window. Light bulbs, table lamps and torches can also be used.

Try to use lighting to produce special effects. Use a torch for spot lights. If you cover a torch with coloured cellophane, you can get coloured lighting, to create different moods.

General Cap-Tin's
THEATRE GROUP

A sample script specially written for the characters in this book

GENERAL CAP-TIN (GCT)

**COOK-CUM-BEARER
FROM TIFFIN TIME (CB)**

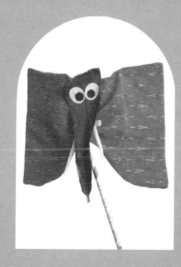

JUMBO (J)

BAT BOY (BB)

SINGING SAINT (SS)

PRIMA DONNA (PD)

DANCING DONKEY (DD)

Curtains open.

Enter CB, J, BB, SS, PD. Lot of talking, laughing and noise.
Enter GCT, with the spotlight on him.
Military drum beat as he enters.

> **GCT: SILENCE!** *(Everyone stops talking.)*
> **"The Hand of Fate". That's the name of the play we are**
> **going to do. And I, General Cap-Tin, am your Director.**
> **Any questions?**

Silence. Long pause, as he surveys the characters. As he looks at each one, the spotlight falls on that puppet, which immediately makes some characteristic movement. E.g: SS sways and hums.

> **GCT: So, this is the cast. A sorry spectacle.**
> **No discipline! No order! I see I shall have to start from scratch.**
> **Before we begin rehearsals, you'll have to learn Discipline,**
> **Obedience and Coordination. Any questions?**
> **Okay, in a line, everybody.**

All shuffle into a ragged line. BB lets himself be pushed into place.

> **GCT: Now. Forward March! One, two, three, four...**

They march to the tune of 'Hup, two, three, four' from The Jungle Book.

> **PD: Stop! This is all wrong.**

Everyone stops and looks at her.
She begins singing and dancing to the tune of 'Ek, do, teen...'.

> **PD: This is the way it goes:**
> **One, two, three, four, five, six, seven...**

Everyone begins to dance with her.
GCT also finds himself dancing, then stops abruptly.

> **GCT: ATTENTION!**

All stand still, except J who keeps bobbing.

> **GCT: You! You with the funny ears!**

> **J: M-m-m-me?!**

> **GCT: Stop swaying! Stop, I say!**

> **J: Can't.**

> **GCT: What do you mean, can't? When I was in the army,**

I had to learn to stand still for hours at a time.
Yes, Sir! Still as a rock!

J: Yessir! S..s..still as a rr..rock!

J sways about and falls off the stage. Others peer downwards.

BB: Looks like he dropped himself, Boss.

GCT: Let him stay dropped. We'll get on with the play.
Never say die, that's my motto! First, salute the flag!

PD: Which flag? There's no flag here.

GCT: What do you mean there is no flag here?
If I say there is a flag, there is a flag. Any questions?

Silence.

GCT: One, two, three... Salute!

*DONG! CB tries to salute, and hits herself
on the head with her plate.*

GCT: You! Spoon-face! What are you doing with that plate?

CB: This is a family heirloom, Sir. My father gave it to me.
My father's dying words still echo in my ears, Sir:
'A cook and his utensils can never ever be parted.'
So I always carry this plate, Sir!

GCT: Too bad. You'll have to be parted from your plate
now that you're in my play.

*Music, while GCT and CB do a kind of dance – GCT tries to get the plate,
CB refuses to give it up. Total chaos. Finally, GCT stops.*

GCT: SILENCE!

Music stops.

GCT: You are fired! I don't want actors with props attached.

CB: Okay Sir, I'm going. I think I will take up my family profession
of cooking, Sir. This drama-shama is not for me. Thank you, Sir.

GCT: (Tearfully) Now will you pleeease make a line
and listen to me?

They line up again.

GCT: Never say die, that's my motto! Clear the stage!

Everyone leaves, except GCT.

> *GCT:* First scene! Any questions?

Silence in the wings.

> *GCT:* Policeman, ENTER!

SS comes in and begins to whirl about, singing a mournful hymn. GCT hops up and down.

> *GCT:* Stop! Stop! Stop!

BB, PD and J enter.

> *GCT:* You're supposed to be a policeman.
> What do you think you're doing?

> *SS:* Policemen carry guns.
> It's against my creed of non-violence.

> *GCT:* But... but... this is a play!

> *SS:* So what? I shall sing my songs of love and peace
> on stage, for all humanity to hear.

SS starts singing and dancing again. GCT sobs in a corner. BB goes to him, and tries to pat him on the back.

> *BB:* There, there. Hymns are all the rage you know.
> He'll be a great hit.

> *GCT:* But... but... but... what about my play?

DD rushes in suddenly. SS stops dancing.

> *DD:* Has anyone seen an eager elephant?

J shakes his head vigorously. The others turn to him.

> *DD:* Ah! There he is! He ran away from the sanctuary.

> *GCT:* An elephant? What's an elephant doing here?
> I thought he was an actor in elephant costume!

> *DD:* No he's an elephant pretending to be an actor.
> He ran off to the city to join the stage.
> Come on Jumbo, let's go.

DD goes off with J.

> *GCT:* Stop, I say! But what about my play?
> Oh, alright. There's no elephant in the play anyway.
> Never say die, that's my motto! Next scene. Everyone out!

All the characters leave.

      GCT: **Sets!**

Two trees pop up, as scenery.

      GCT: **Lights**!

A red light focussed on the stage.

      GCT: **Right! In the park! Heroine! ENTER RIGHT!**
      Villain! ENTER LEFT and kidnap heroine! Any questions?

BB approaches PD from the left. A rope hangs over his shoulder.
PD thwacks him. He falls, out cold.
The red light goes off and normal lights come on.

      GCT: **Blast! Now look what you've done, woman!**
      You weren't supposed to punch him, damn it!
      You were supposed to shout for help!

      PD: **You think I need help against a wiry specimen like that?**
      Huh! I refuse to act in this silly play. It'll ruin my screen image
      as Muscle Maharani, the Avenging Queen.

PD tosses her head, and goes off.
SS begins to sing another mournful song and dances around.

      GCT: *(Snorts)* **Blasted bunch of indisciplined civilians!**
      To hell with the stupid play!

GCT goes off to a side and sits bent.
He watches SS dancing around, and slowly straightens up.

      GCT: **Wait a minute! I can't give up like this.**
      I have it! I'll start a Magical Mystic Band! I'll get the Witch, Spook,
      Mr Big-Ears... Oh yes, it'll be quite a hit. Come on, Saint, old chap.
      Let's go!

Spotlight on GCT as he turns to the audience.

      GCT: **Never say die, that's my motto!**
      See you all at the first show of
      General Cap-Tin's Magical Mystic Band!

They go out. GCT sings a soulful song to a military rhythm,
and marches out.

SS continues on his mournful note.

Growing up with Puppets Unlimited

It was in January 2004 that I first picked up a copy of *Puppets Unlimited with Everday Materials*. I was 11 years old.

Little did I realize then that just over a decade later, I would join Tara Books as a designer myself, and that my first project would be to re-design that very same book!

The first edition of *Puppets Unlimited* was published in 1998 — an outcome of a workshop on puppet-making with a school for differently abled children. It was designed to be printed in black ink on kraft paper; offset printing was still very expensive, especially for a young and independent publishing house like Tara Books. The photographs of puppets were printed separately, and individually cut and pasted by hand into all the 2000-odd copies of the book. It was a tremendous amount of work, but it had a special charm to it.

In 2016, a few weeks into working at Tara, I received the digital files for the original 120-page book in five different parts. The photographs were taken on a film camera, and there were old albums and a box of negatives for me to sort through. Just out of design school, these "old" ways of graphic design were new and amusing to me.

I set about creating a fresh visual language for this project but soon stumbled upon several layers of hidden obstacles. The biggest concern was that the old photographs were of low quality and would not print well.

Creative folks are known to conjure up wacky solutions to stubborn problems, but the solution to this problem was something completely unexpected: we decided to actually make all the puppets featured in the book from scratch. Good-quality photographs could then be taken, which would give the book a different avatar and open up a whole other world of possibilities for its new edition.

For the next couple of months, my colleague and self-proclaimed hand model Rohini Srinivasan and I spent our afternoons digging through piles of all kinds of materials that we collected, borrowed or stole from around our homes and office. Every other day, a quirky character was born – a plastic bottle turned into a donkey, the coconut from yesterday's lunch became an adventurous explorer, and that extra bit of cloth from the tailor down the road was the perfect sari for a fashionable pop star...

In the process of making each puppet, we discovered another issue. While the content was humorous and friendly, we realized that the instructions could be made more comprehensible – an important aspect of a children's activity book. We then began simplifying the text as we went along.

At this point, my role as a designer became multifaceted: I was making puppets and photographing them; editing the photos while keeping a broad yet consistent layout in mind; restructuring the text; and finally, creating a cohesive visual language for all the elements that would go on a page. There were multiple things to constantly keep in mind and I was unlearning and relearning what it was to be a designer. In spite of this complex rhythm we had established, the book still did not look complete. It seemed to lack something.

We soon found the missing piece in the form of Dhwani Shah – illustrator, designer and the newest addition to Tara's design team. Dhwani joined us in this project and brought in another layer of dynamism and storytelling to the book through her delightful illustrations.

While everything seemed to be falling into place, the book was fated to go through many more alterations, delays and road blocks. It took us a whole three years' worth of time and effort from various people to make *Puppets Unlimited* ready to go out into the world once again. And as I write this, it finally is.

This book and I have been on a 15-year-long journey. I grew up with it, and it has grown up with me. I have seen it as a fascinated child, and I see it now as a critical designer. And what a journey it has been!

Ragini Siruguri
Designer
Tara Books • 2019

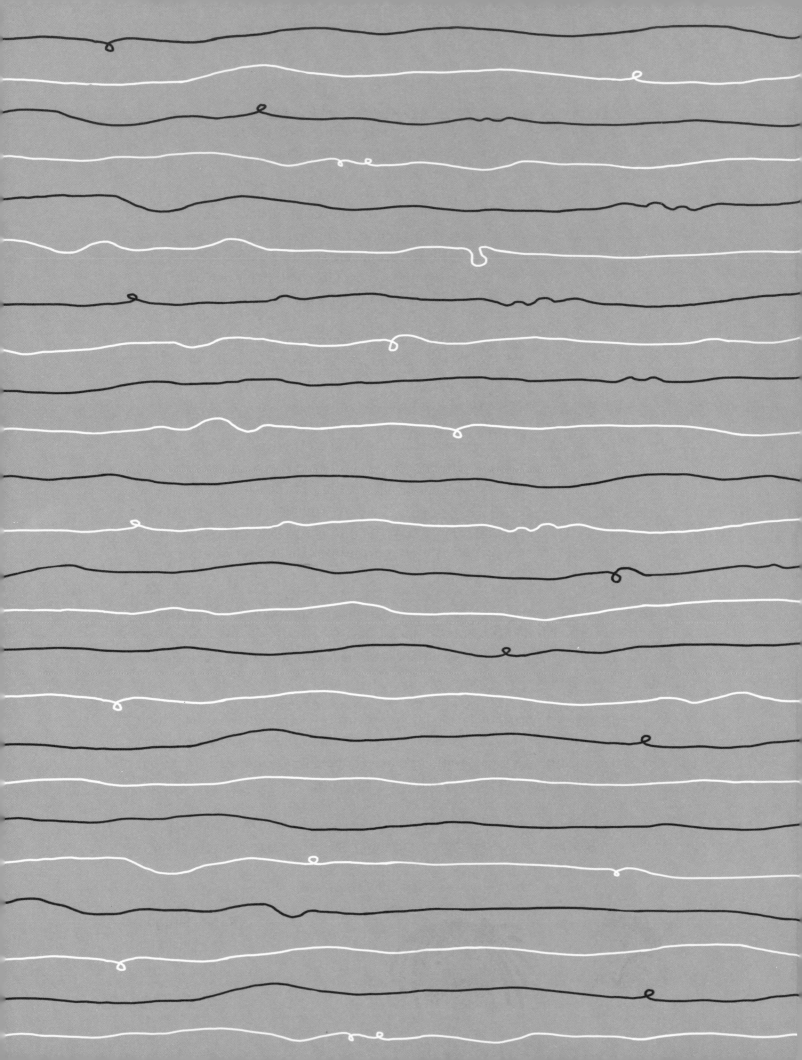